Princess Handbook

Thinks she's a
princess

↘

Susanna Davidson
with help from Princess Beatrice von Preussen

↖

A REAL princess

Illustrated by Mike Gordon
Designed by Hannah Ahmed

Contents

Edited by Lesley Sims

First published in 2006 by Usborne Publishing Ltd., Usborne House,
83-85 Saffron Hill, London EC1N 8RT, England. www.usborne.com
Copyright © 2006 Usborne Publishing Ltd.

CHAPTER ONE

How to be a princess

If you want to be a princess, it helps to be born into the right family. And the right family is a ROYAL family. But even if your parents are just plain Mr. and Mrs. there's no need to panic — you could have been adopted! Your *real* parents, for all you know, could be king and queen of a very exotic country.

You may have a sneaking suspicion you haven't been adopted...

...but don't despair! *Every* girl has the chance to be a princess. Plan B is to find your Prince Charming. If it could work for Cinderella, it can work for you.

In the meantime, you can start preparing for your life as a princess. To be a princess at heart, you must learn to be helpful...

Let me help you.

and polite...

Thank you. Old socks are just what I wanted for my birthday.

...and traditionally, be able to feel a pea under twenty mattresses. (But only very strict and old-fashioned queens still rely on this one – see page 75 for pea-spotting tips.)

The Princess Test

Try this quiz to see if you have what it takes to be a true princess.

1. Your evil stepmother is making you cook and clean for your ugly stepsisters.
Do you:
(a) Work as hard as you can for them?
(b) Do what your stepmother says but complain constantly?
(c) Refuse to do it – after all, that kind of work is for servants?

my stepmother

2. Kidnapped at birth by a wicked witch, you have always dreamed of being rescued by a handsome prince. In the meantime, do you:
(a) Grow your hair as long as it can go. You never know, it might come in useful?
(b) Take up embroidery?
(c) Grow your toenails?

3. You have been forced to leave your palace home after your vile stepmother tried to kill you. Do you:

(a) Go and live with seven dwarfs?

(b) Go and live with three bears?

(c) Move to a luxury pad in the city and take up kung fu, biding your time until you can get your revenge?

4. On your sixteenth birthday you prick your finger on a spinning wheel. Do you:

(a) Promptly fall asleep for a hundred years (without snoring)?

(b) Bandage it up, being careful not to spill any blood on the carpet?

(c) Scream loudly until a servant comes to your aid?

If you answered:

Mostly As: *CONGRATULATIONS!*

You are clearly a princess at heart.

 Mostly Bs: You're on the right track:

you just need to brush up on your fairy tales.

Mostly Cs: Dig deep.

You *really* need to get in touch with your inner princess.

To be a proper princess, you also need to master all the royal rules and regulations. This is where *The Princess Handbook* comes in very handy. If you study it carefully, you'll be picking up princes in no time.

First and foremost, you need to know your way around your palace home...

YUMMY
CAKES

EXOTIC
FRUIT
JUICES

No p(a)lace like home

A princess's palace has everything a girl could desire.

My TV room (with giant screen)

Handsome prince visiting me

My bedroom

My gym

My stables

My servants

And naturally, there's more than one. As well as the main palace, there's the winter castle in the mountains, the royal residence in town and the summer palace by the sea.

A princess knows her homes like the back of her hand: the sneaky back way to the chef's kitchen, the best bannisters for sliding down and most importantly, HIDING PLACES. These should be comfy yet cunning, so you can outwit anyone trying to drag you off to see elderly duchesses with bristly chins.

Where are you, Your Royal Highness? The duchesses are here...

Hiding place

12

The banquet room and ballrooms are mainly used for state occasions, but their polished floors make good skidding surfaces. The mirrored dining hall is also great for rehearsing dance moves.

You can spend your afternoons swimming in the palace pool, or visiting various relatives in their private suites. The most far-flung palace wings are to be avoided though. Your parents will have filled these with your more peculiar relations.

Your bedroom will be crammed full of antiques, beautiful art objects and your very own four-poster bed. Pictures of movie stars are not allowed on the walls (which are usually silk and hand-painted). Try the ceiling of your four-poster instead.

Next to your bed you'll find a number of bells. Each one is connected to a different room in the palace, so you can always alert a servant to your needs. Do you feel a sudden urge for hot chocolate topped with squirty cream and melted marshmallows? Just press that bell and the chocolate is yours...

MUSIC CD

LATEST ISSUE OF PRINCESS WEEKLY

CHOCOLATE

MANICURE

YUMMY ICE CREAM

FRUIT SMOOTHIE

TEDDY

As in most old buildings, ghosts can be a problem. Generations of princesses have lived in your room before you and some of them *will* insist on lingering. These spirits may only be wanting to chat...

When I was alive...

Off with your head!

But princesses have also reported seeing angry queens...

pesky poltergeists...

and persistent princes.

If you want to get rid of your ghosts, try blasting
out some loud music...

...or ignore them in the hope they'll
get bored and go away.

One hundred,
one hundred
and one...

If that doesn't work, you can always move
into another bedroom. After all, there are over
500 of them in the palace.

Your servants

An army of servants is constantly at work to make sure palace life runs like clockwork. Here's a spotter's guide to...

EVERYONE WHO WORKS FOR YOU

First up are your LADIES-IN-WAITING: think best friends and star servants rolled into one. Hand-picked by the queen, they are made up of cousins, duchesses and countesses your own age.

They'll help you out at state occasions, accompany you on trips away and answer any fan mail.

Without your PRIVATE SECRETARY, life would be chaos. He organizes your diary, makes decisions on your behalf and offers advice on how to behave.

BLEURGH!

In China, it's polite to belch during meals... but NOWHERE else.

He is also your link with the outside world, dealing with the press (tricky), keeping you up to date with political matters (boring) and arranging official photoshoots (fab).

Your EQUERRY is a little like a male lady-in-waiting. Usually a senior army officer, he travels around with you, opens car doors for you and generally makes sure your life runs smoothly. Though respectful, equerries are *not* to be messed with. They can be strict and scary and they have eyes in the backs of their heads.

Your DRESSER is a dream come true. She'll ensure you have a wardrobe that makes even supermodels green with envy. She'll accompany you on shopping trips, tell you what's hot and what's not and make sure you're in the right outfit for each occasion.

There are hundreds of other people at work behind the scenes. Here are just a few of them:

Pages - supervise the arrival and departure of your visitors

Housemaids - dust, clean and attend to your every need

Butlers - serve your food and see to the table arrangements

Chefs - the top cooks in the country, who prepare mouthwatering meals

Footmen - help serve your meals, stoke your fires, look after your pets and ride behind carriages at state events

If in doubt about how to behave, try thinking who your ideal princess would be and make her your ROLE MODEL. You could choose a fairy tale princess...

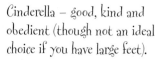
Cinderella – good, kind and obedient (though not an ideal choice if you have large feet).

Snow White – stunning-looking and great at caring for others. But she was slightly dim (after all, she accepted a lot of poisoned goods from her stepmother).

Ariel – okay, so she's a mermaid. But, in spite of her tail, she's still a great role model: brave, beautiful and free-spirited.

Or, you could look to real princesses...

Cleopatra – a powerful princess of Ancient Egypt. She was fantastic at making men do just what she wanted. Think charm, wit and intelligence.

Princess Elizabeth (now Queen Elizabeth II) – a dedicated princess who is devoted to her country and always puts DUTY first. Also a good role model if, like her, you are crazy about animals (especially small dogs).

Princess Haya Bint Al Hussein of Jordan – seriously sporty and hot on women's rights. At the age of thirteen, she represented her country at show jumping and even knows how to drive a truck.

Boarding school

Sadly, you can't just laze around
in the palace all the time.
Modern kings and queens like
to pack their daughters off
to boarding school, to give
them a chance to mix with
"ordinary" people.

Check out the school uniform BEFORE
you agree to go to the school.

If you're shy, you might want to keep the fact that
you're a princess quiet. In which case, when you're
talking with fellow pupils, don't:

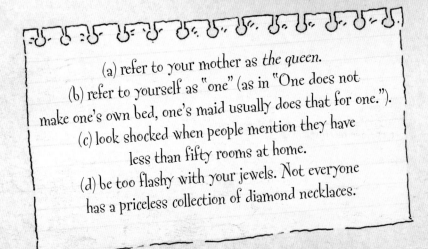

(a) refer to your mother as *the queen.*
(b) refer to yourself as "one" (as in "One does not
make one's own bed, one's maid usually does that for one.").
(c) look shocked when people mention they have
less than fifty rooms at home.
(d) be too flashy with your jewels. Not everyone
has a priceless collection of diamond necklaces.

On the other hand, being a princess at school has its perks. You can:

 snub rude or nasty pupils by not asking them back to the palace for tea.

 impress the cool crowd with your friendships with top fashion designers.

 secure the love of everyone by inviting dashing princes to school parties.

This is my friend, Prince Hunksome.

CHAPTER TWO

How to dress

As a princess, you are a leader of fashion. Of course, your dresser is there to help you, but you still need to develop a style of your own. A natural flair for fashion helps, but without it a princess can still get by — as long as she remembers a few key rules...

26

Fashion do's and don't's:

Do...
(a) buy from the best designers.
They are the most expensive,
but your father, the king,
will understand. If not, ask
your mother to speak to him.
(b) read fashion magazines to keep
up-to-date with the latest look.
(c) brush your hair until it shines
(a tip from Rapunzel) and keep
your teeth a pearly white.

Don't...
(a) cake yourself in make-up.
It can be very unattractive.
(b) buy clothes with logos splashed
all over them. Your style
should be about understatement.
(c) forget to wash behind your ears.
You can only sparkle if you're spotless.

Cheaper clothes, if carefully selected, can look as stylish as designer numbers. To get as much wear out of them as possible, ask your maid to ensure they are always hand washed and ironed. And remember to cut off the labels...

Of course, even the most sophisticated princesses can make mistakes — so learn how to carry them off. Smile, wave at the crowd and hold your head high. As a leader of fashion your mistakes might just catch on.

Everyday wear

For the days when you're not out lunching with foreign princes or launching ships, it's perfectly acceptable to dress down (whatever your grandmother may tell you). Fifty years ago there would have been an outcry if a princess appeared in anything other than a full-on frilly dress...

Her dress only has one bow!

I think I'm going to faint.

Ye Olden Days

...but times have changed. These days, a princess can get away with jeans and flip-flops. BUT (and this is an important "but") a princess should always stand out from the crowd.

Dare to be different

Rule Number One:
don't buy the dream
outfit that's in all the
fashion mags. Everyone
else will be wearing it too.
Go for something similar,
but add your own twist.

Rule Number Two: pay no attention to the saying
"Never wear the same thing twice." The only people who
follow this rule have something to prove – as a
princess, you don't. For variety, try wearing your fave
accessories in different ways.

Rule Number Three: spot the latest trend before everyone else. If you think that's going to be a sombrero, buy one, wear it with pride and enjoy yourself. But as soon as everyone else catches up, move on. A princess should always be one step ahead.

Rule Number Four: a princess should never look scruffy. Remember — even on days off, you are still representing your country. Say "NO!" to designer rips, frayed denim, heavy piercings and tie-dye tops.

Rule Number Five: don't take fashion rules too seriously. After all, you're a princess. You can make your own!

Another way to keep your fashion followers on their toes is by regularly changing your hairstyle. Plus, you'll always be able to find a way out of a bad hair day. Here are a few suggested styles (though of course your stylist will have ideas of her own):

French bun

(be a ballerina for a day)

Ringlets

(very princessy, so a good one for state occasions)

Bunches or pigtails

(cute and casual — but not to be worn with a crown)

Plaits or braids on side of head

(as sported by the inter-galactic Princess Leia)

Pretty hairband

(sweet, demure and elegant — perfect for summer parties)

Big bow in hair

(this one will please your grandmother, so try it at family parties)

Rapunzel

(keep it long for visiting princes)

Out and about

As you grow older, your royal duties will increase. Luckily, so will your wardrobe, as different events demand different outfits...

Walkabouts involve (you guessed it) walking about — and meeting the general public. If you're not known for your grace and poise, don't attempt them in skirts that are longer than you.

Avoid extremely tight skirts too.

I can only take *really* small steps!

Slow coach...

Photoshoots require careful thought. Wear clothes that you know are flattering, rather than trying out something new. If you have any revolting habits, keep them at bay. You don't want to be caught picking in public.

State occasions are *not* the time to try out your new miniskirt and high heels. Who wants relatives patting them on the head and saying how much they've grown?

DAILY NEWS
EXCLUSIVE!
GLAM PRINCESS

Movie premieres are a chance to ooze sophistication. If your mother suggests a smocked dress with puffed sleeves, nod politely and make a private appointment with a top designer.

It's vital that you feel confident of your appearance before leaving the palace. Spend time in front of your wall-to-wall mirrors so you can see yourself from all angles. You could also set up your video camera and film yourself walking, to check your posture and poise.

Finally, don't forget those
small but important details...

Accessorizing

No princess's outfit is complete without a handbag.
As well as adding that finishing touch, it is also the
ideal place to store vital personal items.

Pearl-encrusted
purse

Pocket mirror

Linen
handkerchief

Silver comb

Gold-plated
phone

Don't worry too much about the size of
your bag. Heavy or cumbersome
items can always be carried
by one of your
entourage.

You may want to ask your maid to sew monograms onto your wraps and scarves. This way, if you leave anything behind, it can be returned to you.

Monograms can also be a cunning ploy to capture a prince. Try leaving something "by mistake" at his place. Drape your wrap over a chair or around a statue. The prince then has the perfect excuse to phone you, or even deliver the item in person. If his butler calls instead, you know he wasn't the prince for you.

Come and see the rest of my palace.

Just coming!

Dressing for a ball

Choosing a ball dress takes time, thought and preparation. Start planning at least six months in advance.

Always be firm with the king if he starts quibbling over the cost and make sure he allows you to purchase the finest clothes. It may help to remind him that the better you look, the sooner you can find a handsome prince to marry; and then your father will no longer have to foot your fashion bills.

Make sure you choose a style that suits your shape. Which princess body shape are you?

Princess Victoria (later Queen of Great Britain): narrow top, big bottom. Draw the eye away from the hips with accessories and choose off-the-shoulder necklines to widen your shoulders.

Crown Princess Victoria of Sweden: hourglass figure. Wear well-fitted stretchy-fabric dresses to show off those curves.

Princess Mary of Denmark: tall and athletic. Wear floaty clothes to give a feminine shape and swingy skirts to give a curve to your hips.

Princess Marie Antoinette (later Queen of France): short and slim. Choose off-the-shoulder or floaty baby-doll style dresses to create gentle curves and show off your shoulders. Avoid strappy shoes (these can make legs look shorter).

Princess Anne of Cleves (married King Henry VIII of England): wide body, no waist. Go for muted shades, thin fabrics and avoid clothes with pleats and gathers. Wear high-heels rather than chunky shoes.

Preparing for a ball is of course very tiring, and you want to look your best on the big day. If you're feeling tired, charter your private jet to take you for a relaxing weekend in the Caribbean. If it's hurricane season, make do with the summer palace in the Med.

Choosing your jewels

Young princesses are usually expected to wear pearls, but as you grow older you can begin to delve deeper into your collection of jewels...

It is possible to love jewels so much that one's judgement becomes clouded. A basic rule to remember is that you can wear *either* large earrings *or* an extravagant necklace, but not both together.

The Christmas tree look should be avoided in public.

Then again, when you're alone, it's perfectly acceptable to load on every single jewel you possess and dazzle to your heart's desire.

41

The finest piece in your collection will probably be a tiara. You may own several different styles.

Fringe tiara   Meander tiara   Lover's knot tiara

Sadly, royal rules dictate that you cannot wear any of them until your wedding day.

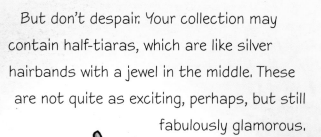

But don't despair. Your collection may contain half-tiaras, which are like silver hairbands with a jewel in the middle. These are not quite as exciting, perhaps, but still fabulously glamorous.

(Pets, of course, don't have to worry about these rules.)

Once you are married and allowed to wear your tiaras, make sure you wear them with care...

A CAUTIONARY TALE

Once upon a time, at the state opening of parliament, two elderly duchesses were engaged in deep conversation. As they bent nearer each other, their spectacular tiaras became locked together, like the antlers of fighting stags.

They were stuck like that for HOURS. The court goldsmith had to be summoned to disentangle them.

CHAPTER THREE

How to move

Being a princess isn't just about wearing pretty dresses and traipsing around in half-tiaras. A true princess must be graceful at all times. Every movement you make, from the turn of your head to the sweep of your curtsey, must be polished and poised.

Gliding gracefully

Do you walk like a peasant or like a princess? Take this test to find out...

1. Try walking with your crown on your head (or a book, if you don't happen to have your crown handy). What happens?
(a) It balances perfectly, naturellement.
(b) It falls off.
(c) I'm not even going to try. I have better things to do with my time, like counting caterpillars.

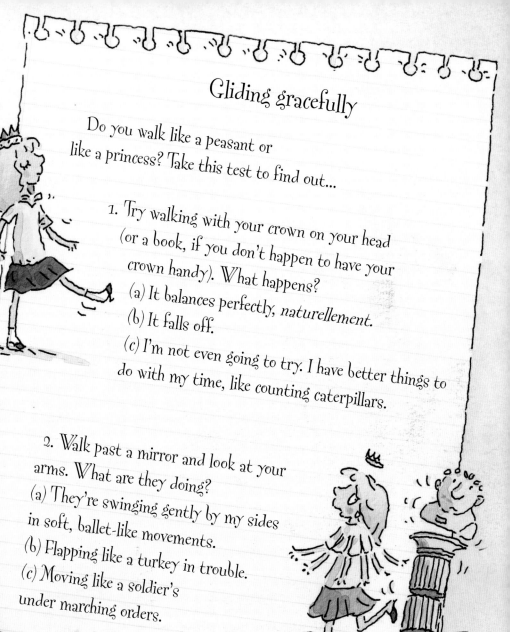

2. Walk past a mirror and look at your arms. What are they doing?
(a) They're swinging gently by my sides in soft, ballet-like movements.
(b) Flapping like a turkey in trouble.
(c) Moving like a soldier's under marching orders.

3. Walk ten steps forward. Where are you now?

(a) Not much further from where I started. I only take the daintiest of steps.

(b) In pain, not having spotted the furniture in the way.

(c) Near to Planet Zog, on the outer rim of the galaxy. My rapid strides mean I cover vast distances in no time.

PLANET ZOG

4. How do you walk down the stairs?

(a) I skip gracefully.

(b) I generally trip, fall, then clutch the bannisters for dear life.

(c) I make the stairs shudder beneath my pounding feet.

Silly girl!

If you answered:

Mostly As: CONGRATULATIONS!
You have the grace of a swan and are already
gliding like a princess.

Mostly Bs: You are a clumsy duckling.
But don't fret, there is still time to improve.
Walk with books on your head and take smaller
steps. Once you can move daintily and silently
in Wellington boots, you'll know you've nailed it!

Mostly Cs: Go back to page 5 of this book and
start again. You are clearly missing the point of
what it means to be a princess.

Running

There is not a huge amount to say about princesses
and running, as the rule is quite simple:
Princesses don't run.
Ever?............... No! Not even if you are being
chased by a fire-breathing dragon or a hairy
spider. After all, you have to give the prince of
your dreams a chance to rescue you...

Sitting down

You might think you know how to sit, but there is an art to this as well.

(a) Keep your knees together.

(b) Cross your legs for the sophisticated look.

(c) Sit with a straight back, with your hands folded neatly in your lap.

Keeping a straight back, often for three hours or more at state banquets, is harder than it looks. The Victorians perfected it by strapping wooden boards onto girls' backs, so they had no choice but to sit up straight. Perhaps try this on your little brother first, to see how effective it is.

Just two more hours to go now.

The curtsey

As a princess, you only have to curtsey to people who are more important than you. In other words, hardly anyone! But you do need to curtsey to the king and queen, even if they are your parents...

Hi Ma'am!

...only on very formal occasions though (or you'd spend your life bobbing up and down). For a quick curtsey, simply put your right foot behind your left leg and bend your knees, while holding out your skirt with your hands.

Naturally, your servants will be curtseying to you. The rule is twice a day — once in the morning and once in the afternoon. So if they've already curtseyed once and you come into a room at 11:55, they needn't worry. But at 12:01 it's time for them to drop their knees again.

It's also polite for a princess to curtsey to foreign royal families. In these situations, hold out your skirt and raise your right hand to be kissed. If you're curtseying to a king, keep your head lowered. (This will make you look sweet and demure.)

When curtseying to a handsome prince, try peeking up at him through your lashes. But if he plants a wet kiss on your hand, lower your eyes at once. You don't want to catch the attention of slobbery princes.

Prince Slobberdink, Your Highness.

Waving

A princess's wave is her trademark. She starts work on it at an early age, and once mastered it need never be changed. Take some style tips from the master-wavers.

The "come-hither" wave: a small, discreet hand gesture performed by gently turning the wrist. As perfected by Queen Elizabeth II.

The "talk-to-the-hand" wave: raised arm and flat palm. Popular with Princess Alexandra of Denmark.

The "elbow-only" wave: involves moving the forearm in a side-to-side sweep. Princess Grace of Monaco preferred this one.

The "eager-waver": no holding back, vigorous shoulder-to-fingertip shake. As used by Princess Mary of Denmark.

CHAPTER FOUR

How to talk

There are three words a princess should remember at all times: *manners, manners, manners.* She must be kind, polite and gracious to everyone, whether plumber or prince. Put your politeness to the test on a younger brother or sister. If you can be polite to them, you can be polite to anyone.

It is especially important to be polite to your servants. Learn their names, ask about their families and *never* snap at them — you don't want to end up like Marie Antoinette (Austrian princess who married the King of France). The French thought she was spoiled and lazy and didn't say "thank you" enough, so they chopped off her head.

The other thing to remember is NEVER gossip. If you are bursting to tell a secret, try writing it down in your Top Secret Royal Diary, or tell your pet...

...unless, of course, it's a parrot.

Meeting and greeting

When meeting the general public, shake hands and smile sweetly at everyone. If you're feeling nervous about an event, work on some secret signals with your ladies-in-waiting beforehand, so they can come swiftly and promptly to your aid.

Signal: Sneezing
Meaning: You've got toilet paper stuck on your shoe.

Signal: Patting hair
Meaning: I've forgotten this person's name.

Signal: Patting hair and sneezing at same time.
Meaning: Don't kiss Prince Ferdinand. He has sweaty cheeks.

Signal: *Hand on hip and sneezing at same time.*
Meaning: *Hide! Your Great Aunt Esmerelda
(with the bristly chin) is looking for you.*

Other royals will call you by your first
name until you're eighteen. After that,
they may change to Ma'am (you may
want to remind them this rhymes with
"jam" not "arm"). Everyone else should
address you as Your Royal Highness.
If people forget, chop off their heads.

Off with
his head!

Only joking. Have a word with one of your ladies-in-
waiting — she'll take the person aside and tell him his
mistake. As mistresses of tact, they can do this
without causing *too* much embarrassment.

Attending events

You will be asked to attend everything from glam parties with Hollywood stars to the opening of village halls and school libraries. You must attend them all with equal enthusiasm (even when it means missing your fave TV show).

If you have to make a speech, keep it short. That way, less can go wrong. When launching ships, don't forget it's customary to refer to the ship as a "she". Using the word "it" is rude, and the word "he" will only cause confusion.

Talking at tea parties

Tea party conversations should be kept light and airy, like the cakes. You should also remember not to raise your voice, and shouting is totally unacceptable, on any occasion, unless it's an emergency.

WE'RE OUT OF CAKE!

Running out of cake, for example, is not an emergency. The ONLY three things you can shout are:

(1) "FIRE!"

(2) "STOP, THIEF!"

(3) "RESCUE ME!" (It's a bonus if you can shout this at handsome princes who are single, wealthy and not in the habit of giving wet kisses.)

Behaving at banquets

Banquets are very important social occasions.
You must be charming, witty and willing to keep the
conversation flowing. As soon as the banquet date
is set, your ladies-in-waiting will study the seating
plan and begin investigating the guests, to make
sure you know what, and what *not*, to say. They will
write down their reports and hand them to you before
the banquet, so you can
study them in depth.

Guest: Princess Aurora (otherwise
known as Sleeping Beauty)*
Hobbies & interests:
sleeping
Good conversation starter:
Boo! (It may wake her up.)
Try not to mention: spinning
wheels (they upset her).

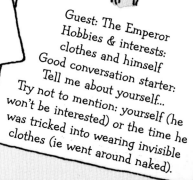

Guest: The Emperor
Hobbies & interests:
clothes and himself
Good conversation starter:
Tell me about yourself...
Try not to mention: yourself (he
won't be interested) or the time he
was tricked into wearing invisible
clothes (ie went around naked).

Guest: Prince Charming^HPA
Hobbies & interests:
ballroom dancing, glass shoes
and girls with wicked stepmothers
Good conversation starter:
I lost a glass shoe the other day....
Try not to mention: the fact you
(a) have big feet or (b) don't have
a wicked stepmother.

Guest: Beautiful Queen (otherwise
known as Snow White's stepmother)**
Hobbies & interests:
poisoning princesses who
are prettier than her
Good conversation starter:
You are looking beautiful today.
Try not to mention: the name Snow
White. It makes her furious.

Guest: Lord Robin of Loxley
(otherwise known as Robin Hood)
Hobbies & interests:
firing arrows and stealing from rich
people to give to the poor
Good conversation starter:
What's the best kind of arrow?
Try not to: draw attention to all the
gold plates and crystal glasses.
He may want to steal them.

Key
* = to be avoided
** = definitely to be avoided
HPA = Handsome Prince Alert

59

On the day of the banquet, it's a good idea to read through the newspapers, so you can sound knowledgeable if asked about current affairs.

Of *course* I know about the situation in Outer Mongolia. Who doesn't?

Also, remember that royal menus are often in French, so brush up on your vocab too. That way, you'll know what you're eating.

Frogs' eyes and sheep's legs?

I think you'll find it's the other way around.

Once you are seated, look to see if the queen is talking first to the man on her left or her right, then follow suit. It's always good to begin by asking people questions about themselves and don't talk about yourself unless prompted. This way people won't get bored — even if you are.

By the third course, it's time to talk to the person on your other side. Sneak a peak at their place card if you can't remember their name.

If the conversation grinds to a halt, smile sweetly and simply ask another question.

Remember, you may ONLY speak to the people sitting on either side of you. *Never* talk over the table to the person opposite you, even if he is the handsome prince of your dreams.

After dinner

Once the meal is over, the queen will stand up and the ladies will follow her out of the dining room. Don't forget to go with them. Staying behind with the gentlemen is a big no-no. The ladies will first go to powder their noses and then sit in the drawing room. This is your chance to discuss the dinner guests, but remember to be discreet.

I think Robin Hood is stealing from us!

How dare you say that! I'm Maid Marian, his wife.

LOOT

If the banquet is taking place in your own palace, slip down to the kitchens at the end of the evening and thank the staff. Not only will this show what good manners you have, you may also be offered helpings of leftover chocolate cake.

CHAPTER FIVE

How to eat

You're at a state banquet and there are three knives in front of you. Which one do you use first? There's a warm bowl of water by your glass. Do you drink it? Where should you put your dirty napkin at the end of a meal? A princess needs to know all this and more. Read on to find out how to handle your plate like a pro.

Knowing your knives

Dining etiquette is actually much less complicated than you might think. There are different knives and forks for each course, but the basic rule is to start on the outside and work your way in.

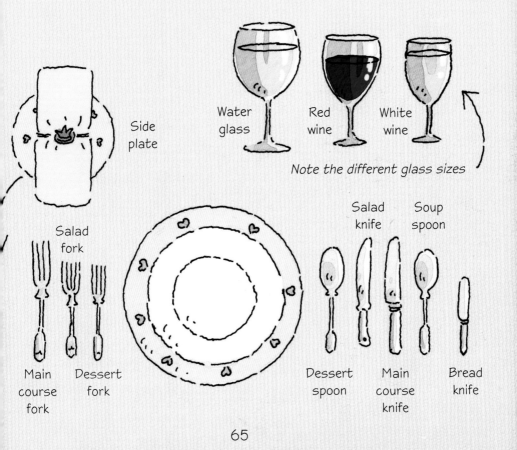

Side plate

Water glass

Red wine

White wine

Note the different glass sizes

Salad fork

Main course fork

Dessert fork

Salad knife

Soup spoon

Dessert spoon

Main course knife

Bread knife

Starters

At the beginning of the meal, wait for the queen to be seated, then sit down yourself. Open your napkin and spread it on your knee. Be careful not to confuse the napkin with the tablecloth.

If you have an evening purse, place it beneath your napkin. You can eat bread with your fingers, but make sure you put butter from the butter dish on your side plate, *not* straight onto your bread.

Soup is often served as a first course. And not your everyday vegetable number either. Royal soup is on a whole different level: think champagne soup or bird's nest soup (a Chinese speciality). When someone serves you, it will be over your left shoulder, so be prepared.

Always acknowledge the waiters and thank them. Tilt the soup bowl away from you (not too far), then tilt your spoon and scoop it up. Don't SLURP or DRIBBLE and definitely don't drink from the bowl.

DRIBBLE!

SLURP!

Main courses

If there's a warm bowl of water next to you with some lemon in it, DON'T DRINK IT! It means you'll be served asparagus (the only thing you can eat with your hands apart from bread) and the bowl is for rinsing your fingers. However, if you see someone else drinking from their finger bowl, that is a different matter... (see below).

A TRUE TALE

Once upon a time, Queen Elizabeth II was at a state dinner. An important guest mistook his finger bowl for a glass of water and drank from it, thirstily. The Queen spotted his mistake and, to save him from embarrassment, she drank from her finger bowl too. Soon, everyone at the table was doing the same.

The main course will
usually be fish or meat,
although vegetarians are
also catered for.

At a really grand event you may even be served
peacock or swan. The most important thing to
remember is that you must eat everything in front of
you, even if it is your absolute worst food. Try to act
as if it's just what you wanted.

If it's your fave food *ever*, try to show some
restraint. Don't gobble it up and NEVER
lick your plate or use your fingers to
swipe up tasty sauce.

Table manners

A list of rules to bear in mind at banquets:

★ Never turn your back on the guests to either side of you. Simply turn your head when talking.
★ When not eating, rest your hands on your lap and don't fiddle with things.
★ At the end of the meal, leave your spoon and fork on your plate and your napkin on your chair.
★ Once you're seated, don't leave the table under ANY circumstances (even if you are BURSTING).

More lemonade, Your Royal Highness?

Top tip: don't drink very much on the day of a banquet and go the loo* *before* the banquet starts.

*That's "bathroom" for all those American princesses out there.

CHAPTER SIX

Marrying a prince

Meet your future husband, darling.

In **Ye Olden Days** finding a prince wasn't a problem.
Arranged marriages were all the rage, so your
bridegroom would have been picked for you at birth.
But these days a girl has to find her prince All By
Herself (sigh). The one good thing about the situation
is that you won't end up with someone old and hairy
who smells of cabbage.

Picking a prince

It's important to remember that some princes are actually in disguise (usually as a result of evil spells cast by wicked witches). The most common disguise is that of the frog prince. To spot your prince, you first have to know your frogs from your toads.

Slimy skin

Frog (but possibly a prince)

Dry skin

Warty

Toad (just a toad)

Once you've found your frog... kiss him! Sorry, this is the *only way* to break the spell. Of course, not all frogs are princes, so you may have to kiss a lot of frogs before you find your prince...

she loves me, she loves me not she loves me....

Other princes have been disguised as bears or beasts. This is much more tiresome: to break the spell you don't just have to kiss them, you have to prove that you truly truly love them, even though they are horribly ugly and hairy. This can take years.

The Princess Handbook suggests you stick to frogs, or better still, pick a prince who is *not* under a spell. There are a number of ways of capturing a prince's undying love and devotion. Here are a few options:

1. Ask your fairy godmother to magic up an amazing outfit and whisk you off to a ball so you can meet the prince of your dreams. If you don't actually have a fairy godmother (a MASSIVE oversight on your parents' part, you need to have words with them) try Option 2.

2. Lock yourself up in a tower so your prince has to rescue you. (He may take a while, so be sure to take a large supply of chocolate cookies with you and your fave books to pass the time.)

3. Pretend you've been asleep for a hundred years. Your princely love will have to wake you with a kiss and then marry you. If you get bored waiting, don't worry. Focus on being a high-powered career princess instead.

BEEN ASLEEP FOR

The Pea Test

If you do find a prince, he may want to check you're a real princess before he marries you. In which case, you'll have to pass the PEA TEST. (This is not to be confused with the PEE TEST, where you have to sit through a really long banquet without going to the bathroom.)

The Pea Test involves feeling a pea under lots of mattresses. This can be tricky, as princes often use old peas that have become mushy and are therefore almost impossible to feel. It's really best to cheat. Basically, if a prince puts you in a bed with more than five mattresses and then asks you how you slept – simply say...

Very badly. There was something HUGE in my bed.

In that case, will you marry me?

Your royal wedding

Dum-dum-di-dum, dum-dum-di-dum... Woo hoo!
You have captured your prince, which means no more
frog-kissing or time spent in towers. Instead, you can
roll out the red carpet and check into your new palace
home. Of course, there are a few things you need to
do first:

1. Choose your tiara
2. Choose your wedding gown
(the longer the train the better)

3. Get married

4. Wave to the admiring crowds from the palace balcony

5. Step (gracefully) into the gold-plated, velvet-cushioned, horse-drawn royal carriage. Then sit back and relax as you're whisked off to live HAPPILY EVER AFTER...

JUST MARRIED!

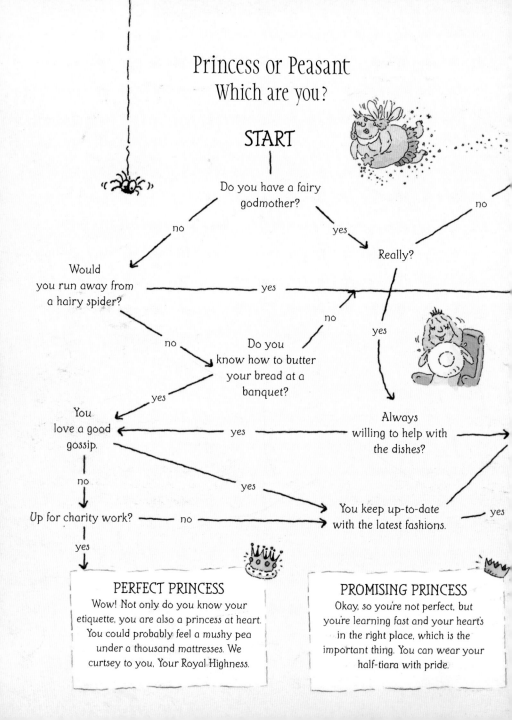

Princess or Peasant
Which are you?

START

Do you have a fairy godmother?

no → Would you run away from a hairy spider?

yes → Really?

no →

Would you run away from a hairy spider?
yes → Really?

no → Do you know how to butter your bread at a banquet?

Really?
no → Do you know how to butter your bread at a banquet?
yes →

Do you know how to butter your bread at a banquet?
yes → You love a good gossip.

Always willing to help with the dishes?
yes → You love a good gossip.

You love a good gossip.
no → Up for charity work?
yes → You keep up-to-date with the latest fashions.

Always willing to help with the dishes?
yes → You keep up-to-date with the latest fashions.

You keep up-to-date with the latest fashions.
yes →

Up for charity work?
no → You keep up-to-date with the latest fashions.
yes → PERFECT PRINCESS

PERFECT PRINCESS
Wow! Not only do you know your etiquette, you are also a princess at heart. You could probably feel a mushy pea under a thousand mattresses. We curtsey to you, Your Royal Highness.

PROMISING PRINCESS
Okay, so you're not perfect, but you're learning fast and your heart's in the right place, which is the important thing. You can wear your half-tiara with pride.

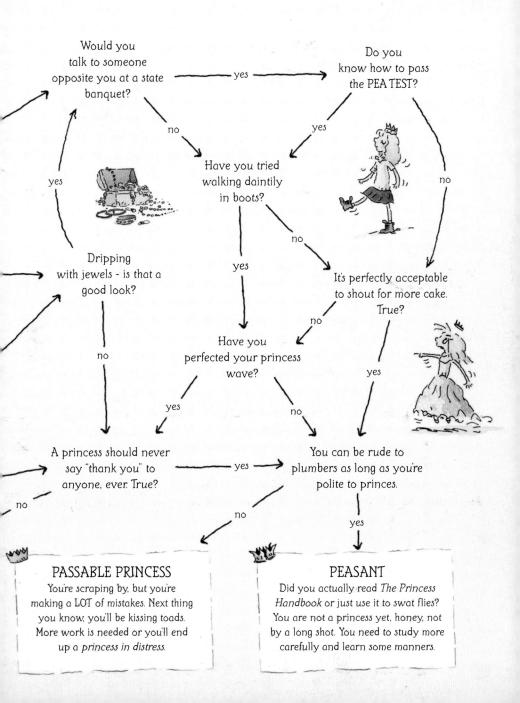

Would you talk to someone opposite you at a state banquet?

— yes → Do you know how to pass the PEA TEST?

no → Have you tried walking daintily in boots?

yes → (Do you know how to pass the PEA TEST?)

no → It's perfectly acceptable to shout for more cake. True?

Dripping with jewels - is that a good look?

yes → (Would you talk to someone opposite you at a state banquet?)

Have you tried walking daintily in boots?

yes → Have you perfected your princess wave?

no → It's perfectly acceptable to shout for more cake. True?

Have you perfected your princess wave?

yes → A princess should never say "thank you" to anyone, ever. True?

no → You can be rude to plumbers as long as you're polite to princes.

It's perfectly acceptable to shout for more cake. True?

no → (Have you perfected your princess wave?)

yes → You can be rude to plumbers as long as you're polite to princes.

A princess should never say "thank you" to anyone, ever. True?

— yes → You can be rude to plumbers as long as you're polite to princes.

no →

You can be rude to plumbers as long as you're polite to princes.

yes ↓

PASSABLE PRINCESS
You're scraping by, but you're making a LOT of mistakes. Next thing you know, you'll be kissing toads. More work is needed or you'll end up a *princess in distress.*

PEASANT
Did you actually read *The Princess Handbook* or just use it to swat flies? You are not a princess yet, honey, not by a long shot. You need to study more carefully and learn some manners.

Index